Grammar Plus!
Activities to Teach and Reinforce Grammar

Grammar Plus!

Capitalization & Punctuation
Grades 4–6

Reinforcing basic grammar skills has never been easier or more fun than with this collection of intermediate-level activities. Whether you're planning for individual students, pairs, or groups, these exciting activities and reproducibles will score big with your students and make planning a cinch. Inside you'll find

- sections on these important skill areas: capitalization; punctuation; and abbreviations, acronyms, initialisms, and numbers
- fresh, new, and practical ideas that are designed especially for the busy teacher
- ready-to-use reproducibles

Editors:
Becky Andrews
Kim T. Griswell
Cindy Mondello

WITHDRAWN

Writers:
Becky Andrews, Carol Felts, Michael Foster, Patricia Twohey, Stephanie Willett-Smith

Art Coordinator:
Barry Slate

Artists:
Teresa R. Davidson, Sheila Krill, Greg D. Rieves, Donna K. Teal

Cover Artist:
Nick Greenwood

Manufactured in the United States N.C. WESLEYAN COLLEGE
10 9 8 7 6 5 4 3 2 1   ELIZABETH BRASWELL PEARSALL LIBRARY

Table of Contents

Capitalization

- Capitalize the **first word** in a sentence.

  EXAMPLE   Another dog ran by the boy.

- Capitalize **proper nouns.**

  EXAMPLE   Billy, New York City, St. Louis Rams

- Capitalize **geographic names.**

  EXAMPLE   Indian Ocean, Hawaii, Empire State Building

- Capitalize the **pronoun _I_.**

  EXAMPLE   He asked if I wanted to read next.

- Capitalize the names of **days** and **months.**

  EXAMPLE   Tuesday, October

- Capitalize the names of national, religious, and local **holidays.**

  EXAMPLE   Memorial Day, Easter, Founders' Day

- Capitalize **proper adjectives.**

  EXAMPLE   French, Kentuckian

- Capitalize **words** used as **names.**

  EXAMPLE   Do you need help, Mother?

- Capitalize **titles** used with names.

  EXAMPLE   General Bradshaw, Mrs. Key, Chief Dann

- Capitalize the **first word** in the **greeting** or **closing** of a **letter.**

> **EXAMPLE**   Dear friends,   Yours truly,

- Capitalize the **first, last,** and **all the main words** in the title of a book, movie, song, magazine, play, newspaper, or television show.

> **EXAMPLE**   *Bridge to Terabithia,* "America the Beautiful"

- Capitalize the names of **organizations, associations,** or **teams** and their members.

> **EXAMPLE**   American Red Cross, Parent-Teacher Organization, Washington Wizards

- Capitalize the names of **businesses** and the official names of their **products.**

> **EXAMPLE**   McDonald's® hamburgers, Colgate® toothpaste

- Capitalize **historical events, documents,** and **periods of time.**

> **EXAMPLE**   Boston Tea Party, Declaration of Independence, Stone Age

- Capitalize **initials** or **abbreviations** that stand for names and also abbreviations of titles and organizations.

> **EXAMPLE**   T. S. Eliot, M.D. (Doctor of Medicine), CIA (Central Intelligence Agency)

Capital Letters Collage

 Capitalizing proper nouns

PROPER		COMMON
Freshen Up	-	detergent
Senator Jones	-	politician
Sparkly	-	polish
Cats Illustrated	-	magazine
Montana	-	state
Fruity-Os	-	cereal

Let art play a part in capitalization practice with this easy-to-do activity! For homework, ask each student to bring in examples of proper nouns from home. Encourage students to cut out examples from empty product boxes, old magazines or newspapers, etc. The next day, have each child glue her examples collage-style on a colorful sheet of construction paper (or have partners or small groups combine their samples to make one big collage). On the back of the collage, have the student list each proper noun and a common noun that describes it. Display the collages in your classroom as a ready reminder of the capitalization all around us.

Proper Noun Subs

Capitalizing proper nouns

Look no further than a favorite story for a great capitalization review! First, select a short story or selection from a read-aloud book. Be sure the selection contains a number of proper nouns. Recopy the selection, substituting each proper noun with a common noun. Underline each common noun that you added; then make a class supply of the rewritten selection. On his copy, direct each student to write an appropriate proper noun above each underlined common noun. When students are finished, read aloud the original selection. Then have student volunteers share their versions. Discuss why each of the common nouns didn't need to be capitalized and why each proper noun did.

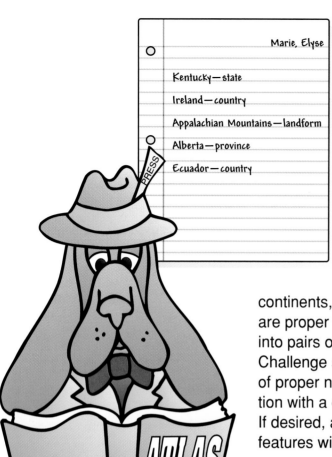

Marie, Elyse

Kentucky—state

Ireland—country

Appalachian Mountains—landform

Alberta—province

Ecuador—country

"Geog-ing" for Capital Letters

Capitalizing geographic names

Send students on a globe-trotting expedition with this activity that focuses on capitalizing geographic locations. First, explain to students that specific geographic locations—continents, countries, states, landforms, public areas, etc.—are proper nouns requiring capitalization. Then divide students into pairs or small groups. Provide each group with an atlas. Challenge students to use the atlas to locate and list examples of proper nouns. Direct students to list the name of each location with a common noun that describes it (see the sample list). If desired, award a small prize to the group that lists the most features within a predetermined time limit.

Alphabet Capitalization

Capitalizing days, months, and holidays

Stop the presses! Here's a capitalization homework assignment that's anything but ho-hum. Give each student a large sheet of white construction paper. First, have the child draw a chart on her paper as shown. Direct her to write rules 5 and 6 from page 14 in the left-hand column as shown. Then have her fill in each blank box along the top with a different letter of the alphabet. For homework, have the student fill in each box on the chart with a sentence that begins with the appropriate letter and illustrates the designated rule. The next day, have students meet with partners to check each other's work. If desired, post the charts on a bulletin board titled "The ABCs of Capitalization!"

	C	P	L	S
Rule 5: Capitalize days and months.	Casey visited me on Tuesday.	Picnics are fun in May.	Last October we went camping.	Sarah's family goes to the movies on Saturday.
Rule 6: Capitalize the names of holidays.	Connie got a doll for Christmas.	Promote good citizenship at school on Presidents' Day.	Lent comes before Easter.	Some wear green on St. Patrick's Day.

Get Wacky With Capitalization

Capitalizing the names of national, religious, and local holidays

Uppercase letters really stand out when your students discover wacky holidays. First, list a few unusual holidays on the board, such as Pretzel Sunday, Rat's Wedding Day, Lazybones Day, and Buzzard Day. Describe these holidays to your youngsters (see the box). Point out the use of capitalization in each holiday. Next, divide students into small groups. Challenge each group to brainstorm a list of wacky holidays. Have each group list its holidays on the board, circling each capitalized letter. As a class, check for correct capitalization in the listed holidays. Invite each student to choose a holiday from the list. Have her write several imaginative sentences about the holiday, including the name of the holiday in each sentence. After students exchange papers to check capitalization, have each student write each corrected sentence on a separate sentence strip, highlighting the capital letters by tracing them with a marker. Display the finished strips on a bulletin board or classroom wall titled "Wacky Holiday Capitalization!"

REAL WACKY HOLIDAYS

Rat's Wedding Day
On the 19th day of the first lunar month, some Chinese families go to bed early to give the rats plenty of time to play! They leave food out for the rats to keep them from devouring the food in the family's kitchen.

Lazybones Day
On one special day of the year, young people in the western Netherlands whistle, bang on pots and pans, and ring doorbells to wake up their neighbors. But they don't get in trouble for it. In fact, any youth who doesn't wake up to join in the noisemaking gets the title "Lazybones" or "Lazy Lak." The original Lazybones was Piet Lak, a night watchman who fell asleep and failed to warn his countrymen of French invaders.

Pretzel Sunday
In Luxembourg, boys present their sweethearts with yummy decorated pretzel cakes before Easter. If the girl likes the boy, she gives him a decorated egg on Easter Sunday. The bigger the pretzel cake is, the bigger the egg must be!

Buzzard Day
Even the homely buzzard has a day of its own. On March 15, when the turkey buzzards come home to roost in Hinckley, Ohio, the locals flip a few pancakes, share some arts and crafts, sell souvenirs, and listen to talks by naturalists.

All About Me!

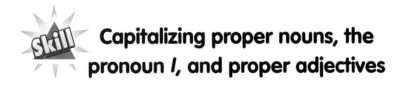

Capitalizing proper nouns, the pronoun *I*, and proper adjectives

Extra! Extra! Here's a capitalization activity that's perfect for your next writing workshop. First, have each child write a paragraph about himself—without mentioning his name—that includes at least five examples of correct capitalization illustrating rules 2, 4, and 7 from page 14. On the back of his paragraph, have the student list each capitalized word and explain why it is capitalized. Collect the paragraphs. Then read one aloud. Challenge the class to first identify the student being described. After the class meets this challenge, reread the paragraph and ask students to determine which words require capitalization and why. Repeat until each student's paragraph has been read.

To Capitalize or Not to Capitalize

Skill **Capitalizing words used as names**

All of your students will win new writing skills with this capitalization challenge. Write each of the words in the box at left on a separate index card. Place the cards in a paper bag. Have a student volunteer draw one card from the bag and write a sentence on the board, using the word in a sentence. Have him pass the card to another student. This student writes a sentence that uses the word as a name. The student then chooses a different student to draw the next card from the bag. The challenge continues until each student has had an opportunity to write a sentence. As a class, check all sentences for correct capitalization.

Once your students have met the challenge, reward them with a tasty letter-filled treat. Mix together a box of Alpha-Bits® cereal and a large bag of M&M's® candies. Give each student a small paper cup filled with the treat.

aunt	mother
brother	officer
chief	professor
dad	sister
daughter	son
general	teacher
grandmother	uncle

On a First-Name Basis

 Skill **Capitalizing titles used with names**

What's in a name? Plenty of capitalization practice! Give each student a large sheet of white construction paper. Have the student turn the paper vertically and write her first name down the left margin in large, fat bubble letters as shown. For each letter, have her use a pencil to write a sentence that begins with that letter and illustrates capitalization rule 9 (see page 14). Remind her to capitalize titles used with names and to keep them lowercase when not used with names. When finished, direct each student to swap papers with a partner for checking; then have her trace over her corrected sentences with a fine-tipped marker. Finally, have her decorate the letters in her name with colorful markers, crayons, or pencils. Display the completed name posters on a bulletin board titled "What's in a Name?"

King George loves horses.

Admiral Sealey runs a tight ship.

You were once the king of England, but now you're not.

Lieutenant Smith came to speak to our class.

After he left office, the former president gave speeches at schools.

"Dear Singing Sensation,..."

Skill **Capitalizing the first word in the greeting or closing of a letter and titles used before names**

For an activity that's guaranteed to deliver loads of fun capitalization practice, try this letter-writing idea. First, ask each child to label an oaktag strip with a topic of interest; then have her decorate the strip. Post the strips as a border around a bulletin board. Next, have students cut out magazine and newspaper pictures of famous personalities. Mount each picture on the bulletin board with a name card. Then have each student choose one personality and write him or her a letter about one of the display's topics. Require that the student include at least five capitalization errors related to rules 9 and 10 (see page 14) in her letter. On the back of the letter, have the student write an answer key. After students share their notes, pin each letter on the bulletin board. During free time, challenge each student to take a letter from the display, list its capitalization errors on her own paper, and then turn the letter over to check.

Capital Book Reviews

Skill **Capitalizing book titles and proper nouns**

Want the scoop on how to turn your next book report assignment into a capital way to practice capitalization? First, write rules 11 and 2 on the board (see page 14). Give each student two large blank index cards. On one card, have the student write a brief review about his book that includes at least five capitalization errors related to the book's title or a proper noun. Direct him to write an answer key on the back of the card. Next, have the student decorate the other card with a new cover design for his book. Have him tape his two cards together as shown to create a minibook. Collect the minibooks and distribute them randomly to students. Direct each child to read the review and list each capitalization error on his paper, along with the number of the rule that it illustrates. When students are finished, have them return the minibooks to their owners, along with their papers for checking. At the end of the activity, place the minibooks in your classroom library so students can refer to them when looking for a new book to read.

I read <u>sarah, Plain and tall</u> by patricia macLachlan. It won the newbery medal in 1986. It is about a woman from maine who answers an ad for a wife. She comes to marry anna and Caleb's dad, Mr. wheaton. They all hope she will love them. I thought this was a great book.

Sarah, Plain and Tall

by Patricia MacLachlan

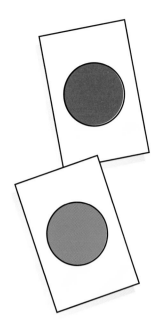

Red Light, Green Light!

Skill **Capitalizing the names of businesses and the official names of their products**

Find out in a flash how well your students understand capitalization with this simple activity! Give each student two large index cards. On one card, have the student draw a large red circle. On the other card, have her draw a large green circle. One at a time, display one of the sentences below on the overhead. Point to a word in the sentence; then ask each student to raise her green card if the word needs to be capitalized and the red one if it doesn't.

SENTENCES

My favorite candy bar is the baby ruth®.

When I go to mcdonald's, I always order a large fry.

Do you drink dr. pepper®?

I ship all my packages with federal express.

For my birthday, my mom bought me a nintendo® at toys "r" us.

My little brother has a slinky®.

Sometimes we shop at wal-mart.

Junk Mail Capitalization

Skill **Capitalizing the names of organizations, associations, teams, businesses, and products**

Don't throw away that mountain of junk mail you get every day—turn it into a teaching tool with this capitalization activity! Bring in appropriate examples of junk mail. Also ask students to donate samples from home. Place the junk mail in a plastic grocery bag. Next, give each student (or student pair) a copy of page 14 and a highlighter pen. Ask each child to reach into the bag without looking and pull out one or more pieces of junk mail. Then challenge the student to read her mail to find examples of capitalization that illustrate rules 12 and 13. Direct her to highlight each example and label it with the applicable rule. Provide time for students to share some of their samples. Then, if desired, write rules 12 and 13 on large index cards. Post them in the middle of a bulletin board titled "Capitalization Rules!" Have students staple their highlighted junk mail collage-style around the poster.

A Brief History of Capitalization

 Capitalizing historical events, documents, and periods of time

Dig into the past and discover a treasure trove of free-time capitalization practice. In advance, draw a large, open treasure chest on yellow bulletin board paper. Label the chest "Capital Treasures." Cut out the chest and mount it on a bulletin board. Next, write capitalization rule 14 (see page 14) on a sentence strip. Staple the strip above the treasure chest. Place old newspapers and history-related magazines, scissors, construction paper, pushpins, and glue near the display. During free time, have students search through the newspapers and magazines to find examples of the posted rule. Direct students to cut out each example, glue it to construction paper, and then pin it in or around the treasure chest. Reward each student who helps fill the chest with several gold-foil-wrapped chocolates.

Capitalize historical events, documents, and periods of time.

A Novel Idea

 Using capitalization rules

Add capitalization practice to your reading workshop with this simple idea. As you read aloud a selection in a story or novel your class is currently reading, stop periodically when you encounter a capitalized word. Ask students to list the word in their reading journals and write a sentence telling why it is capitalized. (Place a sticky note on the book's cover so you can list the words to use later for checking.) At the end of the reading period, check to see if students correctly identified the capitalization rules illustrated by the words.

Capitalization Center

Using capitalization rules

If you like having plenty of independent activities on hand for your students, try this idea! Make copies of several magazine articles, short stories, and letters. Glue each onto a sheet of construction paper. Then highlight and number several capitalized words in each selection. Below the selection, include a numbered blank for each capitalized word as shown. On the back of the sheet, provide an answer key. Laminate the sheets; then place them in a basket with a wipe-off marker and some paper towels. When a student visits the center, he chooses a selection to read. Then he reviews the highlighted words and writes in the appropriate blank why each is capitalized. After the student checks his work with the answer key, have him wipe the sheet clean so it's ready for the next classmate.

Four Corners Capitalization

Using capitalization rules

Give capitalization rules a real workout with this "standing room only" game! In advance, list four capitalization rules on the board (see the list on page 14). Give each student four index cards. On each card, have the student write a sentence that uses capitalization according to one of the rules listed on the board. Collect the cards and check them for accuracy. Then write the four rules on numbered sentence strips as shown. Post each strip in a different corner of your classroom.

To play, give each student a sentence card. At your signal, have each child move to a corner according to the capitalization needed in his sentence. Have each student, in turn, read his sentence aloud and explain why the rule applies to it. If the student is in the wrong corner, challenge his classmates to help him select the correct one. After all students have shared, roll a die. If 1–4 is rolled, have students standing in the corresponding corner sit down. If a 5 or 6 is rolled, let all students remain standing. Then collect the cards, distribute new ones, and play another round. Continue until you run out of cards or only one student is left standing.

1. Capitalize geographic names.

We visited the Astrodome in Houston.

Do you think the spacecraft landed on Mars?

Picture-Perfect Capitalization

 Using capitalization rules

The French racer passed the racer from Spain. (1, 2, 7)

The leader of the race was Speedy Sanchez. (1, 2)

The next big race will be held on October 25. (1, 5)

Look at that guy go, Dad! (1, 8)

The winner will be interviewed on <u>Larry King Live</u>. (1, 11)

Try this group activity to help students learn and apply capitalization rules. Have several students cut out interesting pictures from old magazines (at least one per cooperative group). Glue each picture to the top of a 12" x 18" sheet of white construction paper as shown. Then give each student group a picture and a copy of page 14. At your signal, challenge each group to write as many correctly capitalized sentences about its picture as it can, making sure to use as many different rules from page 14 as possible. Require that the group list the applicable rule number(s) at the end of each sentence. After five or ten minutes, have each group share its sentences. Award one point for each correct use of capitalization; subtract a point for each capitalization error. Then reward each member of the winning group with a handful of Alpha-Bits® cereal. To use the magazine pictures again, just cut out each one and glue it to a new sheet of white paper.

How About "Dot"?

 Using capitalization rules

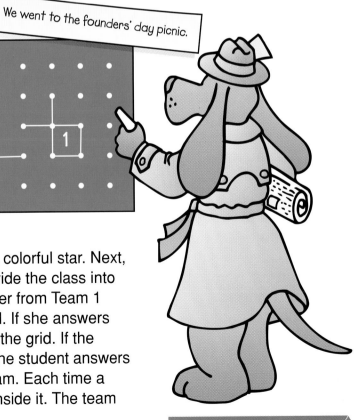

We went to the founders' day picnic.

For a great capitalization review, you can't beat this game—and 'dots' the truth! In advance, write each of 25–30 sentences needing capitalization on a separate sentence strip. (Check in textbooks or teachers' guides for sample sentences, or have students provide sample sentences of their own.) On the backs of five to seven strips, draw a colorful star. Next, draw 25 dots on the chalkboard as shown and divide the class into two teams. Display a sentence; then ask a member from Team 1 to identify the word(s) that needs to be capitalized. If she answers correctly, let the student connect any two dots on the grid. If the strip is starred, let her connect any three dots. If the student answers incorrectly, pose the sentence to the opposing team. Each time a team completes a box, write the team's number inside it. The team with the most boxes at the end of the game wins.

Read All About It!

CAPITALIZATION RULES

Want the scoop on how to make sure your writing is just right? One way is to use capital letters correctly. Be sure to always capitalize the following:

① the first word in a sentence
Another dog ran by the boy.

② proper nouns
Billy, New York City, St. Louis Rams

③ geographic names
Indian Ocean, Hawaii, Empire State Building

④ the pronoun *I*
He asked if I wanted to read next.

⑤ names of days and months
Tuesday, October

⑥ names of national, religious, and local holidays
Memorial Day, Easter, Founders' Day

⑦ proper adjectives
French, Kentuckian

⑧ words used as names
Do you need help, Mother?

⑨ titles used with names
General Bradshaw, Mrs. Key, Chief Dann

⑩ the first word in the greeting or closing of a letter
Dear friends,   Yours truly,

⑪ the first, last, and all main words in the title of a
book: *Bridge to Terabithia*
movie: *Beauty and the Beast*
song: "America the Beautiful"
magazine: *Sports Illustrated for Kids*
play: *Death of a Salesman*
newspaper: *The Wall Street Journal*
television show: *Who Wants to Be a Millionaire*

⑫ names of organizations, associations, or teams and their members
American Red Cross
Parent-Teacher Organization
Washington Wizards

⑬ names of businesses and the official names of their products (but don't capitalize a general descriptive word like *hamburgers* when it follows the product name)
McDonald's hamburgers, Colgate toothpaste

⑭ historical events, documents, and periods of time
Boston Tea Party
Declaration of Independence
Stone Age

⑮ initials or abbreviations that stand for names; also abbreviations of titles and organizations
T. S. Eliot
M.D. (Doctor of Medicine)
CIA (Central Intelligence Agency)

What a Zoo!

The editor of the local newspaper, the *Redwood Reader,* is on vacation. While she's gone, she needs you to proofread an article written by one of her reporters, Lenny Lowercase. Lenny writes great articles, but he often gets so excited about his story that he forgets to use correct capitalization.

Directions: Read the article below. Circle each word that should be capitalized. Then write the word correctly on the numbered line at the right. The first one has been done for you.

Redwood Zoo Goes Bananas
by Lenny (lowercase)

This weekend it really was a zoo at Redwood zoo! After the zoo closed on friday evening, a worker accidentally left the door to the chimpanzee cage open. The zoo's two chimps, bert and ernie, got loose. when the zookeeper, Ann imal, arrived on Saturday morning, they were nowhere to be found. Later that morning, a visiting french zookeeper named Zo e. Ology noticed that one of the reptile cages was empty. The zoo's prized boa constrictor was missing. Apparently the chimps decided to unlatch the cage and let the animal out.

Just like any other Saturday in october, visitors began arriving at the zoo at 9:00 in the morning. The animals were still nowhere to be found. Ann, Zo, and the other zoo workers continued to look for them. Just as they were preparing to call sheriff Al Ert for help, they heard a loud scream from the nearby burgertime restaurant. A woman named ada Lot went to place her order only to find a pair of chimps staring at her from the drive-through window. Apparently the chimps had found a way into the restaurant and helped themselves to the food inside. When interviewed, mrs. Lot said, "All i wanted was a biscuit for breakfast!" At the time this article was written, the boa constrictor was still missing. A search throughout Redwood county is planned.

1. _Lowercase_____
2. _____
3. _____
4. _____
5. _____
6. _____
7. _____
8. _____
9. _____
10. _____
11. _____
12. _____
13. _____
14. _____
15. _____
16. _____

Bonus Box: Write a newspaper article about the search for the missing Komodo dragon. Leave out the capital letters. Then challenge a classmate to circle the words that need capital letters.

Take Note!

Directions: Divide a sheet of paper into six columns. Cut out each notepad and glue it at the top of a column. Cut out each pencil (save the blank ones for later). Then read the sentence on each pencil and underline the word or words that need capitalization. Finally, glue the pencil in the column labeled with the matching rule.

My editor is in a meeting at the empire state building.

The newspaper is full of grocery store ads the week before thanksgiving.

There will be no business section on christmas day.

The article about senator Jones was on the front page.

That article on cooking was written by carolyn ames.

Our main competitor is the *daily gazette.*

Copies of the newspaper are sent to chicago, new york, and miami.

Magazines such as *weekly news* are sold alongside our newspaper in newsstands.

The sale advertisements are in the paper on thursday.

I read chief Garrison's report on a salary increase for police officers.

The sports section is edited by sammy slider.

The newspaper celebrates its 100th anniversary in july.

names of people

geographic names

names of days and months

titles used with names

titles of written work

names of holidays

Bonus Box: On each of the three blank pencils, write a sentence that uses capitalization. Glue each pencil under the matching rule.

©2000 The Education Center, Inc. • *Grammar Plus!* • *Capitalization & Punctuation* • TEC2313 • Key p. 47

Note to the teacher: Provide each student with a 12" x 18" sheet of construction paper, scissors, and glue. If you prefer that notebook paper be used instead, have each student make three columns on the front of a sheet and three on the back.

"A-maze-ing" Delivery

What a mess! Big Al, the delivery truck driver for the *Town Tribune,* was sick yesterday. A substitute took over his route, but the sub got mixed up and dropped off Big Al's papers in the wrong location. Help Big Al find his papers so he can complete his delivery for the day.

Directions: Place your pencil on START. To locate the newspapers, use your pencil to link the words or phrases in the maze that need capital letters. When you're finished, list each word on a line below using correct capitalization.

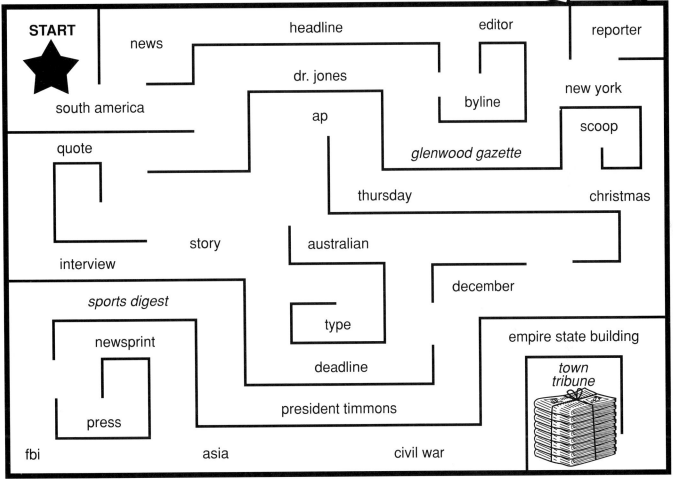

START
news   headline   editor   reporter
south america   dr. jones   new york
            ap   byline   scoop
quote   glenwood gazette
            thursday   christmas
story   australian
interview   december
sports digest
newsprint   type   empire state building
                            town tribune
deadline
press   president timmons
fbi   asia   civil war

1. _____   9. _____
2. _____   10. _____
3. _____   11. _____
4. _____   12. _____
5. _____   13. _____
6. _____   14. _____
7. _____   15. _____
8. _____   16. _____

Bonus Box: On the back of this page or on another sheet of paper, write the letter Big Al wrote to his boss explaining why the delivery was late yesterday. Include at least four examples of capital letters.

It's News to Me!

Directions: Read the words or phrases on each newspaper machine. Circle the one that needs capitalization. In the box on the machine, rewrite the word correctly. Then rearrange the underlined letters in the circled words to fill in the blanks below.

1. brooklyn bridge
   catalog
   soccer

2. my father
   taxi cab
   new york

3. ernest hemingway
   national holiday
   relief map

4. lois lane
   festival
   team leader

5. internal revenue service
   parade
   grocery store

6. ymca
   public pool
   government

The ___ ___ ___ ___ ___ ___ ___ ___ gives the writer credit for a newspaper story.

7. capital
   steamship
   yellow river

8. election
   ontario
   restroom

9. prescription
   december
   weekday

10. book digest
    movie critic
    classified ads

The ___ ___ ___ ___ of a newspaper story answers questions for the reader.

Bonus Box: Write an imaginary newspaper headline that includes three examples of capitalization. Below the headline, explain why each word or phrase is capitalized.

Punctuation

Punctuation includes the following marks: apostrophes, colons, commas, dashes, ellipses, exclamation points, hyphens, parentheses, periods, question marks, quotation marks, and semicolons.

- Use an **apostrophe** to show possession, to take the place of missing letters in contractions, and to form the plurals of letters and numerals.

  EXAMPLE   Sam's best friend never got straight A's, but Sam didn't care.

- Use a **colon** after the greeting in a business letter; to introduce a list; between numbers in time; and to introduce an important quotation in a report, essay, or news story.

  EXAMPLE   Dear Sir: Here are the rules: no gum, no baseball caps, no talking.
  The police officer stated: "We found the suspect's fingerprints at the scene of the crime."

- There are many uses for **commas.** For a listing, see the reproducible on page 32.

- Use a **dash** to separate and stress elements in a sentence. Use after an interrupted or unfinished statement or thought or to introduce a list of items. Use after an introductory list. Also use before and after comments inserted into a sentence to give information or add emphasis.

  EXAMPLE   The cafeteria—and no other room—may be used for school lunches.
  You'll need three things—a pencil, an eraser, and a ruler.
  Toys, hairbrushes, chewing gum—these items must be left at home.

- An **ellipsis** is three dots in a row. It is used to replace words that have been left out. Use an ellipsis to indicate that something has been left out of the middle of a sentence. If something is left out at the end of a sentence, use a period and then an ellipsis.

  EXAMPLE   Mary, Mary...how does your garden grow?
  Four score and seven years ago our forefathers brought forth this nation....

- Use an **exclamation point** after strong interjections, exclamatory sentences, and strong imperative sentences.

  EXAMPLE   Sarah! Get off that desk immediately!

- Use a **hyphen** to break a word between syllables at the end of a line, in two-part numbers from twenty-one to ninety-nine, in spelled-out fractions, and in some compound nouns and adjectives.

  EXAMPLE　　Four-fifths of the twenty-two drive-in movies in town have closed.

- Use **parentheses** to give the reader added information. Also use before and after an abbreviation or an acronym of a company or organization once its full name has been written.

  EXAMPLE　　Read the first story (pages 4–7) tonight.
  　　　　　　　A representative from Trans World Airlines (TWA) will visit our class.

- Use a **period** at the end of a declarative sentence, at the end of an imperative sentence that doesn't require an exclamation point, and after most initials and abbreviations. Also use as a decimal point.

  EXAMPLE　　Dr. A. C. Ross will visit the clinic today.

- Use **quotation marks** before and after a direct quotation or to set off words or phrases used in a special way. Also use before and after the names of book chapters, essays, short stories, songs, poems, and magazine and newspaper articles.

  EXAMPLE　　Sue said, "Pass the paper, please."
  　　　　　　　Cory hummed "Row, Row, Row Your Boat" as he washed the car.

- See page 38 for a list of rules and examples for using **semicolons**.

Contraction Countdown

Skill Using apostrophes in contractions

Practice placing apostrophes in contractions with this exciting game. Divide the class into two teams. Direct each team to brainstorm a list of contractions and the words that form them. Then ask a Team 1 student to call out from his team's list two words used to form a contraction, such as *they are*. Challenge a Team 2 player to write the contraction on the board. If the contraction is written correctly, award Team 2 one point. If the contraction is written incorrectly, give the point to Team 1. Then let a player from Team 2 call out two words for a Team 1 student. (Keep a list of the contractions used on the board so that none are repeated.) Continue until all word pairs from each team's list have been used.

Pockets of Possessives

Skill Using apostrophes in possessive nouns

Samuel	shoe
cars	faces
dog	cookie
trees	leaves
mice	eyes

You'll pocket plenty of independent practice with apostrophes in this activity! Label each of three manila envelopes with one of the following: "Nouns," "Possesses," and "Finished." Then give each student two white index cards. On one card, have the student write a common or proper singular noun (for example, *Samuel*). On the other card, have her write a common or proper plural noun (for example, *cars*). Collect the cards and place them in the "Nouns" envelope. Next, give each student two colorful index cards. On each, have the student write a singular or plural noun that could be possessed by a noun she wrote on a white card (for example, *dog* and *engines*). Place these cards in the "Possesses" envelope. Finally, place all three envelopes in a basket at a center and post the following directions:

1. Select five cards from the "Nouns" envelope. Arrange them in a column on the tabletop.
2. Select five cards from the "Possesses" envelope. Match each card to a white card on the tabletop.
3. For each pair of cards, write a sentence using an apostrophe to correctly show possession. For example: *Samuel's dog chased my cat. The cars' engines are powerful.* Don't worry if a sentence is silly. Just be sure the apostrophe is used correctly.
4. Place your paper in the "Finished" envelope. Return the white cards to the "Nouns" envelope and the colorful cards to the "Possesses" envelope.

1. Samuel's shoe was full of sand.
2. The cars' faces in his cartoon were silly.
3. The dog's cookie was shaped like a bone.
4. The trees' leaves were yellow.
5. The mice's eyes were beady.

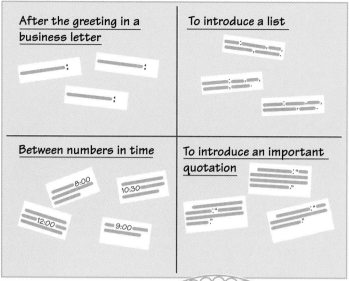

After the greeting in a business letter	To introduce a list

Between numbers in time	**To introduce an important quotation**

Colon Quest

 Reviewing uses of colons

It's a bird! It's a plane! No, it's a colon! Hunt down this important punctuation mark with this group challenge. Divide the class into several teams. Give each team an 18" x 24" sheet of construction paper, scissors, and a glue stick. Direct the team to divide its paper into four sections and label each with a colon use (see page 19). Then set out a supply of old newspapers and magazines. Challenge each team to cut out sentences that use colons and glue each one in the matching section of its paper. Allow several days to complete the activity so students can scavenge for colons at home, too. At the end of the challenge, award five points for each correct example. Then reward each member of the winning team with an edible colon: two Oreo® cookies arranged on a small paper plate. Who knew punctuation could be so sweet?

Semiprecious Semicolons

Using semicolons

To practice using semicolons, try this gem of an idea! After introducing semicolons to students, divide the class into pairs. Give each twosome a copy of page 38 that has been duplicated on white construction paper. On scrap paper, have each pair write two sentences to illustrate each rule listed on page 38. After checking the sentences, direct the pair to use a fine-tipped pen to label each shape with one of its sentences. Then instruct the twosome to lightly color each shape, cut it out, and tape it onto a piece of yarn to make a necklace. Hang each pair's necklace on a bulletin board.

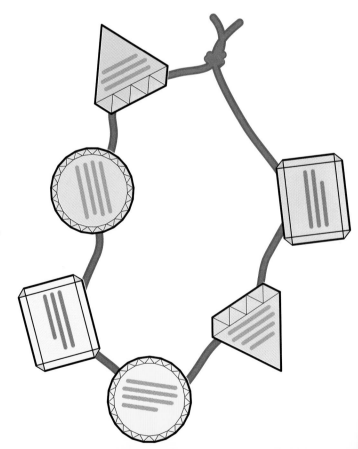

Pass the Commas, Please!

Skill **Using commas to separate items in a series and adjectives that modify the same noun**

Serve up extra helpings of comma practice with this activity! Divide the class into groups. Give each group a paper plate and a topic, such as *food, tools, animals, places, careers, famous people, sports,* etc. Have each group label its plate with its topic and a comma character that illustrates it (see the example). Then instruct the group to use colorful markers to label the plate with nouns related to the topic.

Next, direct each student to use words from her team's plate to write two sentences: one that uses a comma to separate items in a series and another that uses a comma to separate adjectives that modify the same noun. After each student has written her two sentences, have groups swap plates. Then challenge each child to write two more sentences using the topic and words on the new plate. After swapping plates several times, have students share some of their sentences and discuss whether commas were used correctly. Then display the plates and sentences on a bulletin board titled "Pass the Commas, Please!"

Classmate Comma Challenge

Skill **Reviewing uses of commas**

For a quick practice session on using commas, try this easy-to-do activity. Divide the class into groups. Give each group a copy of the comma rules on page 32. First, challenge the group to write five to ten sentences that each illustrate a different rule. Then have the group copy its sentences, omitting the commas, onto a transparency. In turn, ask each group to display its sentences on the overhead. Then have group members call on classmates to add the missing comma(s) to each sentence and explain why it is needed. Save the transparencies to review commas anytime during the year.

The 12 Days of Commas

 Reviewing uses of commas

Want to give your students a noteworthy reminder of comma rules? Cut out 12 large comma shapes from colorful paper and number them 1–12. Then tape a copy of the rules shown behind each cutout. Next, divide the class into 12 small groups and give each group a cutout. Then have groups sing the rules in order to the tune of "The 12 Days of Christmas." Before you can say "Do re mi," your kids will know their comma rules note for note!

The 12 Days of Commas

On the first day of grammar class, I used a comma…

1. to separate three or more items in a series
2. to separate adjectives that modify the same noun
3. between a city and a state
4. between the day and year in a date
5. after the greeting and closing of a friendly letter
6. before a conjunction between independent clauses in a compound sentence
7. after a dependent clause at the beginning of a sentence
8. after introductory words or mild interjections at the beginning of a sentence
9. to set off the name of a person being spoken to
10. to set off an appositive
11. with words that interrupt a sentence's basic idea
12. in quotations

Make a Dash for It!

 Skill **Practice using dashes**

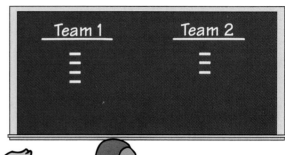

Make a dash for this fast-paced game when you want to practice using dashes! First, review the rules for using dashes. Then have each student write a sentence that includes one or more dashes. After a classmate proofreads her work, have her use an overhead pen to rewrite the sentence, *without* the dash(es), on a small piece of transparency material. Collect the sentences and divide students into two teams. Then place two desks at the front of the room on either side of your overhead projector. On each desk, place a small bell or other noisemaker. Also label a space on the board for each team to keep its score.

To play, call a student from each team to stand behind a desk with her hands behind her back. Display a sentence. The first student to ring her bell and tell where to correctly place the missing dash(es) wins a point and draws a dash on her team's scoreboard. If a student is incorrect, give the opposing player a chance to answer. Continue playing until all sentences have been used. The team with the most dashes on its scoreboard is the winner.

The Dot Squad

Skill **Knowing when to use a period before an ellipses**

Do your students get confused about when to use an ellipsis (three dots) alone or with a period (four dots)? Help clear the confusion with this simple mnemonic device. Tell students to think of the ellipses as the "Dot Squad." This squad likes to march into sentences and replace words with dots. Then tell students to imagine that the commander of the Dot Squad shouts out "Front and center!" (three words) when he wants to replace words at the center (middle) of a sentence. When the commander wants to replace words at the end of a sentence, he calls out "March to the end!", a four-word command, indicating that the writer should end the sentence with four dots. Now, isn't "dot" simple?

Get the Point!

Using exclamation points to add emphasis

Get the point across about using exclamation points with this nifty activity that doubles as a cool display! After introducing the rules for using exclamation points, give each pair of students two pieces of construction paper: a 12" x 18" piece and a nine-inch square. Have students round the edges of the larger piece to make the top of an exclamation point. Then have them round the corners of the square piece to make a circle. Direct the twosome to label the circle with their names and the top part with three sentences—one to illustrate each rule for using exclamation points. After students share their sentences, mount the cutouts on a "Get the Point!" bulletin board.

USES OF PARENTHESES

- to give the reader added information
  Don't forget to read chapter 6 (pages 33–39).
- before and after an abbreviation or acronym of a company or organization once its full name has been written
  We saw a movie about the National Aeronautics and Space Administration (NASA).

Sideways Smiles

Using parentheses to add information

Here's a zany—and effective—way to help students remember how and when to use parentheses. First, have each student draw a large picture of his smiling face on a 6" x 9" sheet of paper. Pair students. Then have partners turn their drawings sideways, slide them apart, and tape a sheet of notebook paper between them as shown. Tell students to think of parentheses as sideways smiles. Then review the uses of parentheses shown at left. Finally, challenge each pair of students to write on their lined paper several silly sentences that use parentheses correctly (see the examples). Provide time for twosomes to share their sentences. Bet you'll see miles of smiles!

Hyphen Hunt

Skill **Using hyphens in compound words**

Sometimes a hyphen is used in compound words. It can also be used to make some new words that begin with *self, ex, great, all,* or *half* or that end with *elect* and *free*. Send students in search of these special words with this group activity. For each group, write the following words on index cards (one per card): *all, hand, in, star, to, step, by, down, me, well, self, earth, known, done, president, read, help, do, aunt, know, it, great, baked, sugar, drive, fifths, purpose, four, esteem, half, thirds, two, free, eight, sixty, elect.* Give each group a set of cards; then challenge group members to combine the cards to make as many hyphenated words as possible, using a dictionary to help. (See the key shown.) Tell students that they may repeat words within a hyphenated word, such as in *step-by-step*. At the end of the time limit, have each group share its list by taking turns announcing one hyphenated word at a time. If a word is on another team's list, have each team's recorder strike it from his group's list. Reward the team with the most words left on its list with a small prize or class privilege.

ANSWER KEY

hand-to-hand	two-thirds
step-by-step	four-fifths
down-to-earth	drive-in
hand-me-down	know-it-all
well-known	sixty-eight
great-aunt	well-done
half-baked	well-read
all-purpose	well-to-do
self-esteem	self-help
sugar-free	all-star
president-elect	

half   known   done   sugar   baked   well   free

Hyphen Karate

Skill **Using hyphens to break words into syllables**

Breaking up doesn't have to be hard to do—at least not in this activity on using hyphens! After introducing the rule on using hyphens to break words between syllables at the end of a line, give each student a ruler, a colored pencil, and a copy of a page from a textbook or novel. Direct the student to measure one inch from the right side of her copy; then have her use the colored pencil to draw a vertical line on her paper as shown. Next, have the student write on her paper each multisyllabic word that the line runs through, using a hyphen to show correct syllabication. (Have dictionaries handy for this step.) After students finish their lists, provide time for them to share some of the words they hyphenated. For more practice, have students swap pencils. Then direct each child to draw a different colored line two inches from the right side of her paper and repeat the exercise.

Period Patch

Skill Using periods correctly

Want to help students cultivate skill in using periods correctly? Give each child a lidded margarine tub, glue, scissors, black construction paper, construction paper scraps, and seven strips of paper. Then have her follow these steps:

1. Trace the lid onto the black paper. Cut out the tracing and add a funny face as shown.
2. Glue the cutout onto the lid's top.
3. On each of seven strips, write an unpunctuated sentence that is missing at least one period. Number each strip 1–7.
4. Write an answer key on a separate sheet of paper and glue it to the bottom of the tub. Put your sentences inside the tub.

Place the tubs on a shelf labeled "Welcome to Our Period Patch!" Then challenge each student to take a tub during free time, rewrite each sentence correctly, and check his work with the key. Or distribute the tubs randomly as a ten-minute filler.

1. Please pass the paper to me

4. I just read a book by C S Lewis

The Period Invitational Tournament

Skill Practice using periods

Kids having a ball with periods? It can happen with this fun activity! Just follow these simple steps:

In advance:
1. Number 18 margarine tubs 1–18. (Use the ones from the "Period Patch" activity above.)
2. Make a copy of page 36's answer key (found on page 48). Cut apart the sentences. Tape each one to the bottom of its matching tub.
3. Give each child a paper bag labeled with his name, and a copy of page 36. Have the student complete page 36 as directed.
4. Divide the class into groups. Give each group a beanbag or soft ball and a six-foot piece of string.
5. Set up the tubs in an open area to resemble a golf course. Beside each tub, place a cup filled with bingo chips (periods).

To play:
1. Start each group at a different tub, or "hole" (for example, start groups at holes 1, 5, 12, and 17). Have each student carry his bag, completed copy of page 36, and pencil.
2. At each hole, the group checks the bottom of the tub for the answer to that numbered sentence on page 36. If correct, a student places a period from that hole's cup in his bag. Next, the group uses its length of string to measure six feet from the tub. Each student gets two chances to earn another period by tossing the beanbag into the tub. Then the group moves to the next hole.
3. Continue until each group has completed all 18 holes. Then add up each student's periods to determine the winner(s).

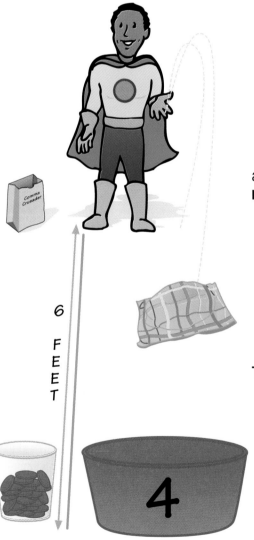

6 FEET

Silence Is Golden

Skill **Punctuating dialogue**

You'll take note of your kids' skills with quotes after this quiet-as-a-mouse activity! With the class, brainstorm a list of five conversation topics. Write the list on the board. Then divide the class into pairs. Have each pair select a topic and write it at the top of a sheet of paper. Then direct the pair to converse about the topic *without* talking! Direct one partner to start off by writing on the paper what she'd like to say as if it were a conversation in a story (for example, "I think shopping is a great hobby!"). Then have her pass the paper to her partner, who reads what is written, skips a line, and then responds in writing. Instruct twosomes to continue this silent conversation until each student has written five separate pieces of dialogue. Then have partners check each other's work for correct use of quotation marks.

Rules for Writing Quotations

Put quotation marks before and after what a person says.

Quotable Quotes

Skill **Introducing the use of quotation marks in dialogue**

Introduce using quotation marks in dialogue with this hands-on activity. Divide the class into groups. Challenge each group to cut out ten examples of dialogue from old newspapers and magazines. Then have the students highlight each speaker's exact words. Next, challenge each group to study its examples and then create a list of rules for writing quotations. Hold a sharing time during which groups share their rules and combine them to make one class list. After the class list is completed, share with students the rules listed on page 20 so they can compare their ideas with the actual rules.

Apostrophe Picnic

Think punctuation is no picnic? Think again! To use an apostrophe correctly, just remember these easy-to-remember rules.

Use an apostrophe:

- to show that a letter or letters have been left out of a word to form a contraction
  do not = **don't**   would have = **would've**
- to show possession
  The **dog's** dish is empty.   The **boys'** soccer team won today.
- to show the plural of a letter or number
  All the **A's** are red.   Find the **8's** and circle them.

Directions: Use the rules above to color the picnic tablecloth below. If the apostrophe is used correctly, color the square with a red crayon. If the apostrophe is used incorrectly, write the correct use in the square. You'll know you did a "f-ANT-astic" job when you see your grade magically appear on the tablecloth.

1. I do'nt like broccoli.	2. How many C's in *cackle?*	3. The cat's collar is tight.	4. She wrote two 12's.	5. They would'nt stop arguing.
6. Do you know if theyr'e cousins?	7. Kana's pen is brand-new.	8. Jims' hat fell off.	9. It is now six o'clock.	10. The captains' jersey is blue.
11. Her jack-o-' lantern is great!	12. Max wasn't at the party.	13. Gus's game is over.	14. We've been waiting for you.	15. That childrens' book is new.
16. Write six 15s' on your paper.	17. I've never been to Paris.	18. Shes' my best friend.	19. Pat and Mike's house is big.	20. The'yll be here soon.

CONGRATULATIONS! Your grade is _____!

Bonus Box: If you could have a picnic with anyone in the world, whom would you choose? Explain your answer in a paragraph that uses at least three apostrophes.

Calling All Colons!

If you want to be a powerful punctuation pro, then you must learn how to put a colon in its place! Read these rules on how to use a colon correctly.

A colon is used after the greeting in a business letter. **Dear Ms. Kline:** **The model car I purchased from your company is missing a tire. The store manager said....**	A colon is used when writing the time using numbers. **The game begins at 3:00 on Saturday.**
A colon is used to introduce a list. **I'll need the following art supplies for art camp: paintbrushes, paints, chalk, art paper, a ruler, markers, and colored pencils.**	A colon is used to introduce an important quotation in a serious report, essay, or news story. **President Lyndon B. Johnson made this statement about peace: "If we are to live together in peace, we must come to know each other better."**

Directions: Find a partner. Then follow these steps together to make a mobile that shows you know how to put a colon in its place!

1. Cut two large circles from construction paper. Each partner writes his or her name on one circle, using fancy or special lettering.

2. Study the four examples above. Then write each rule at the top of an index card.

3. Choose one of the topics below. On the bottom half of each card, write a sentence related to your topic that is an example of that card's rule.

4. Tape the cards and circles together on a length of yarn as shown. Hang your mobile in the classroom.

Topics

Music Videos Weird Animals Dumb Television Shows Teenagers

Bonus Box: Find four examples of colon use in books or magazines in your classroom. For each example, write the rule, title of book/magazine, and page number. Show your list to two classmates. Have them sign your paper if they agree that the examples show how to use a colon correctly.

Note to the teacher: Each pair of students will need a copy of this page, four index cards, scissors, construction paper, yarn, transparent tape, a pencil, and crayons or markers. If desired, award extra-credit points to students who complete the Bonus Box activity.

The Comma Crusader

If using commas correctly is your plan, then the Comma Crusader is your man! Help this punctuation powerhouse place commas correctly by following these rules.

Use a comma:

to separate three or more items in a series
Marge loves spinach, brussels sprouts, and asparagus.

to separate adjectives that modify the same noun
The loud, beeping buzzer woke me up.

between a city and a state
St. Louis, Missouri

between the day and year in a date
February 18, 2000

after the greeting and closing of a friendly letter
Dear Montel,   Yours truly,

before a conjunction that joins the independent clauses in a compound sentence
I tried to call you on Saturday afternoon, but your line was busy.

after the dependent clause at the beginning of a complex sentence
When it began to rain, I knew our picnic would be canceled.

after introductory words or mild interjections at the beginning of a sentence
Yes, you can borrow my new CD. Oh, I didn't know that the test was today.

to set off the name of the person you're speaking to
Jennie, can you have dinner at my house tonight?

to set off an appositive (a noun or phrase that renames or further identifies the noun it follows)
Mrs. Tyra, my math teacher, won the teaching award.

with words that interrupt a sentence's basic idea
**Dad, of course, had to brag about our soccer team to everyone.
Eddie, therefore, will have to leave the game early.**

in front of a short, direct quotation in the middle of a sentence
Callie asked, "Is that your uncle sitting over there?"

at the end of a direct quotation that is a statement when it comes at the beginning of a sentence
"Mrs. Howard is giving a luncheon today," explained Mom.

Command Those Commas!

How do you take charge of punctuation when you write? One way is to command those commas!

Directions: The letter below is missing 34 commas. Read the letter. Add the missing commas using a colored pencil. Command those commas!

Aye-Aye!

708 Martin Street
Albion Illinois 03928
April 5 2000

Dear Grace

   Hi! Even though you are coming for a visit in a few weeks I couldn't wait to tell you what happened the other day. My 14-year-old brother the practical joker had planned all these dumb tricks to play on me for April Fools' Day. It didn't turn out the way he planned however because I was ready with some tricks of my own. First he got up early, took all my dolls, and hung them in the tree in the front yard. He then got in the shower. Well I went out and hung a big bright sign in the tree. It was labeled "Jason Gray's Dolls on Special Display!" Boy was he surprised when all his friends were in the yard laughing it up! He hurried and pulled it down. He was so mad!

   The next trick he tried to pull was after school. He told me that Max the new boy from down the street called and wanted me to call him back. He gave me the number and walked down the hall but I knew he was hiding around the corner to listen. I knew of course that it was a trick to embarrass me. I dialed my friend named Beth. She has an older sister whom Jason is *gaga* over.

   I said "Hello this is Janet. My brother told me you called."

   Beth said "Oh really? What's he up to?"

   I could hear my brother laughing down the hall but I tried not to smile. I replied "Welcome to the neighborhood Max." Beth caught on to Jason's trick so we chatted for a minute while she pretended to be Max. My brother was still laughing. I said in a loud voice "Oh my brother? Your sister wants to talk to my brother?" Jason ran around the corner.

   Beth got her sister on the phone. I told Jason that Max's older sister thought he was cute and wanted to talk to him. Jason took the phone. His voice squeaked out "Hello?"

   Well you should have seen his face when he realized who was on the other end of the phone! I could see he was mad so I started running before he got off the phone and tried to kill me. It was better than pizza ice cream and a big birthday check!

See you soon
Janet

Bonus Box: Write a letter from Jason to one of his friends. In the letter, tell Jason's side of the story. Be sure to use commas correctly.

Dashing Through Sentences

When do you make a dash for a dash? Use dashes:

- to introduce a list of items
There are four things every superhero needs—a partner, a hot car, super-human powers, and a cool name.
- after a list of items that begins a sentence
Trees, cars, houses—all were blown away by the storm.
- after a thought or statement that is interrupted or unfinished
I love being the Dynamic Dash, but—
- before and after questions, comments, exclamations, or other interrupters that give information or add extra emphasis
The police officers—Lieutenants Murphy, Jones, and Solieski—were very brave today.

Directions: Add dashes to the following sentences. Then follow the directions below.

1. Pizza cheese or pepperoni will be served for lunch.

2. Bring the following items to the picnic a dessert to share, a game to play, a swimsuit, and a towel.

3. You will need six items for art class colored pencils, markers, paintbrushes, chalk, a sketch pad, and a ruler.

4. Jason he's my best friend is sleeping over next weekend.

5. Each team wore a special tournament shirt yellow or green for the play-off game.

6. You can do one of five acts for the talent show a dance routine, a song, a short skit, a joke-telling session, or a poetry reading.

7. My wallet in case you hadn't noticed is missing.

8. Lions, tigers, zebras, elephants all can be found at the city zoo.

9. The police chief she's my aunt's sister will speak to my class next week.

10. The scientists say that dinosaurs are extinct, and yet

11. For the field trip you will need these items a bag lunch, a signed permission slip, a jacket, money for the boat ride, and your journal.

12. Soda pop orange, grape, or root beer will be served at the party.

13. Our favorite team the awesome Foxville Fighting Falcons is sure to win.

14. By June you will have learned the following decimals, multiplication, fractions, ratios, percents, and division.

15. The following students should report to me Jamie, Ali, Becca, Kelly, Devin, Susan, Douglas, and Flo.

Use the key provided by your teacher to check your work. If you punctuated a sentence correctly, color the dash. Count up the colored dashes. Color the dash below that shows your total score.

11 or less ☐	**12–14** ☐	**15** ☐
Need some extra help? Dash to your teacher.	You're dashing toward becoming a punctuation pro!	Dynamic Dash Champ

Parentheses Puzzler

Directions: Read each sentence and add the missing parentheses. Then write the letter under each parenthesis in order on the lines below to find out why these dinosaurs are so delighted.

1. There is a number to call if you need help with homework 800-GET-HELP .
   A   E   B   T   I   H

2. The National Broadcasting Company NBC owns Channel 10 .
   S   C   E   Y   E   P

3. The Society for the Prevention of Cruelty to Animals SPCA meets today .
   M   T   A   O   J   U   L

4. Look for information about volcanoes in chapter 3 pages 23–35 .
   K   U   L H   S   T

5. Rosie Mallory my neighbor is running for state senator .
   V   W   I   O   N   P

6. Mom works for the Federal Bureau of Investigation FBI .
      A   C   F   N   T

7. The snake we found was 60 inches five feet long .
      R   O   H   Y   E   B

8. Akeema's native country is Kenya from which he moved when he was eight .
   I   A   Z   D   J   I

9. Fold the paper to resemble a butterfly see the example .
         T   G   N   O

10. Our school Rosewood Elementary has 362 students and 20 teachers .
    E   S   M   A   Y   F

11. The team members in the photo from left to right are Jane, Tina, and Moesha .
    O   N   U   A   R   O   B

12. I had a 12-ounce 355 ml box of juice for lunch today .
         N   T   U H   B   V

13. My father who was late for work searched everywhere for his glasses .
         G   O   P   K

14. I hope my favorite team the Dallas Cowboys® goes to the Super Bowl® .
    L   B   F   W   A   T

15. I've read my favorite book *Tuck Everlasting* six times already !
    U   A   R   M   S

__ __ __ __   __ __ __   __ __ __   __ __   __ __ __ __ __ __

__ __ __ - __ __ - __ __ __ !

Bonus Box: Write a letter to a friend describing the dinosaur tug-of-war you just watched. In your letter, use parentheses at least three times.

Let's Hear It "Fore" the Period!

Want a chance to play for the PGA (Periods Are Great Association)? Then take a swing at these sentences that are just begging "fore" some periods!

Directions: Add a period (and some capital letters) to the sentences below. Color each flag after you finish its sentence.

Use a period:
• at the end of a statement or at the end of a command that doesn't require an exclamation point
• after most initials and abbreviations
• as a decimal point and to separate dollars and cents

1 > Please pass the salt thank you for your help

2 > Sheriff Wayne D Cates investigated the robbery and caught the thieves

3 > My grandfather, Maurice O DeMars, won't tell anyone his middle name

4 > Shanille's mother sent $3 50 to school for the field trip

5 > It will be raining this afternoon we'll postpone the cookout

6 > The sign read "This way to Mississippi St University," so we turned the car around

7 > John F Kennedy was a popular US president

8 > Tony spent $5 32 on baseball cards for his collection

9 > I was surprised to find out that P J Thomason was a girl

10 > Pay $5 00 to the ticket collector and go into the movie

11 > Take out the garbage do the dishes

12 > That golfer on television is Mrs Pugh's nephew, Homer

13 > Where was Michael J Fox born?

14 > Give me the $2 25 you owe me for buying your lunch, please

15 > Dr Flynn lives in Florida she saw an alligator in her backyard

16 > The soccer team practices on Saturday they practice in all kinds of weather

17 > I heard Ms Conway wrecked a golf cart last Friday

18 > The dog dug a hole for his bone he dug it up later in the day

Bonus Box: Write a short speech explaining why the period should receive "Punctuation Mark of the Year" honors this year.

Everybody's Talkin' About—What?

What *are* those three buddies gabbing about? Listen in on their conversation by completing this page on using quotation marks correctly.

Remember: Use quotation marks before and after a direct quotation. Think of them as helping hands that hold a speaker's exact words. To help you know where to put quotation marks, try underlining the speaker's exact words first. Then place the quotation marks before and after each underlined part.

"That sounds like fun," Kim said. "Can I come, too?"

Part One: In the box at the right, three friends are having a conversation. First, underline the exact words that each person is saying. Then add quotation marks.

Part Two: On the back of this page or on another sheet of paper, draw a picture of what you think Micah's birthday gift was. Don't show your picture to anyone until directed to by your teacher.

Hi, Pat and Lea, said Micah.

Hey, Micah, Pat said. What's up?

Micah answered, You won't believe what my grandmother gave me for my birthday!

What? Lea asked.

Guess, Micah responded.

Well, Pat said, how about giving us a few hints?

Good idea! Lea agreed.

Okay, Micah answered, smiling. Let's see. It's something I've always wanted.

That's not much of a clue, Pat laughed. It could be anything.

It's something I'll have lots of fun with, Micah added.

Lea said, That narrows it down to about a million things! Add some details.

Micah continued, It's about 10 inches high and 20 inches long. It feels good to touch. It uses a lot of energy. I'll have to take good care of it. I can keep it in my room. Now, guess what it is. It's a _____!

Lea and Pat said together, It's a _____!

Bonus Box: Make a poster that gives the rules for using quotation marks to write conversation. Illustrate the poster and display it in your classroom.

Note to the teacher: When everyone has completed this page, ask students to share their pictures and support their answers.

37

Semiprecious Semicolons

Use a semicolon:

- to join independent clauses in a compound sentence without a comma and a conjunction
  One cousin is driving here from Colorado; another will take a plane from Maine.

- before some conjunctions that join two simple sentences into one compound sentence. Use a comma after the conjunction.
  He cooked a huge dinner; therefore, he invited the neighbors over.
  Molly is usually right on time; however, today she was late.

- to separate a series of items when one or more of the items include commas
  The art supplies we need for class are paintbrushes; red, yellow, and blue paint; a sketch pad; a charcoal pencil; a calligraphy pen; and an art smock.

Directions: On scrap paper, work with your partner to write two sentences that illustrate each rule above. Proofread the sentences. Then label each gem below with a sentence. Lightly color each gem and cut it out. Then tape the gems onto yarn to make a necklace of your semiprecious semicolon sentences!

©2000 The Education Center, Inc. • *Grammar Plus!* • *Capitalization & Punctuation* • TEC2313

Note to the teacher: Use with "Semiprecious Semicolons" on page 22. Provide each pair of students with scissors, a fine-tipped black pen, a two-foot length of yarn, tape, and crayons or markers.

38

Mechanics

The nuts and bolts of writing—things that may seem small but which can lead to big problems for readers—are called mechanics. They include capitalization (see pages 3–18), abbreviations, acronyms, initialisms, and numbers. These handy tools will turn your students into writing mechanics masters!

- An **abbreviation** is a shortened form of a word or phrase. You usually place a period at the end of an abbreviation, but in some cases you don't.

  EXAMPLE   Ms. Phipps drove 50 mph to get to the PTA meeting by 9 P.M.

- An **acronym** is a word created by using the first letters of a group of words. Acronyms never use periods and are usually written in all capital letters.

  EXAMPLE   PIN = personal identification number

- **Initialisms** are formed from the first letters of expressions or the names of things. They are pronounced one letter at a time. Like acronyms, initialisms are usually capitalized. Initialisms sometimes use periods, but not always.

  EXAMPLE   CIA = Central Intelligence Agency

- There are several rules for writing **numbers** correctly:
  — Numbers from one to nine are usually written as words; numbers 10 and above are usually written as numerals.

  EXAMPLE   The last six students only had 20 minutes to finish the test.

  — Very large numbers may be written as a combination of numerals and words.

  EXAMPLE   Over 5 million fans attended the concert.

  — Numbers being compared should be written in the same style.

  EXAMPLE   Each team should have 3 to 12 players.

  — When beginning a sentence with a number, use words instead of numerals.

  EXAMPLE   Twenty students competed in the race.

  — Use only numerals when writing page or chapter numbers, addresses, dates, time, money amounts, decimals, percentages, and statistics.

  EXAMPLE   Tonight's homework is on page 6 in chapter 2.

Wiped Out!

 Writing abbreviations

Want to spy your students writing abbreviations correctly? Then try this fast-paced game! In advance, write on an index card each unabbreviated word listed. Place the cards facedown in a stack and divide the class into two teams lined up in front of the chalkboard. Draw the top card and show it to the first student in each line; then say "Go!" Each of these two players dashes to the board, writes the card's word, and then hands a chalkboard eraser to the next teammate before going to the back of the line. (If necessary, tape the card to the board so students can copy the word correctly.) The next player goes to the board and erases one letter that is omitted when the word is abbreviated. When all of the required letters have been erased, the next player adds a period and circles the abbreviation to signal that the answer is complete. If a player makes a mistake (such as writing a word incorrectly or erasing the wrong letter), the next player must use her turn to correct the error with her team's help. The team that correctly abbreviates a word first earns a point. Continue play until all of the cards are played or time runs out.

EXAMPLES

Word	Abbreviation
Mister	Mr.
Doctor	Dr.
Senior	Sr.
Junior	Jr.
Street	St.
Road	Rd.
Avenue	Ave.
August	Aug.
Department	Dept.
inches	in.
quarts	qt.
page	p.
Drive	Dr.
Boulevard	Blvd.
pint	pt.
Apartment	Apt.
Parkway	Pkwy.
Mountain	Mt.
Company	Co.
Incorporated	Inc.

In the News

 Identifying abbreviations, acronyms, initialisms, and numbers

Highlight the use of abbreviations, acronyms, initialisms, and numbers with this fun-to-do newspaper activity. Provide each group of two or three students with a section of a newspaper and four different-colored markers: red, green, yellow, and blue. Set a timer for ten minutes; then have each group search its newspaper and highlight items according to this code:

abbreviations = red
acronyms = yellow
initialisms = green
numbers = blue

At the end of the time period, tally the number of each item correctly highlighted by each team.

Crazy States

State abbreviations

State abbreviations are no big deal with this crazy card game! For each group of four students, cut 26 index cards in half to make 52 cards. Write each alphabet letter—capital letters only—on two cards. Also make a copy of the list of state postal abbreviations for each group. Place one 52-card deck and an abbreviations list in a manila envelope. Then give one envelope to each group, along with the following directions for playing.

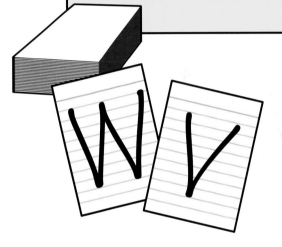

How to play (two to four players, plus one dealer):
1. Choose one student to be the dealer. The dealer deals the cards and checks all abbreviations with the answer key.
2. The dealer deals two cards to each player and then places the deck facedown on the table.
3. Player 1 checks her cards. If she cannot make an abbreviation, play passes to the next player. If she can make a state abbreviation from her cards, she places them faceup on the table to be checked by the dealer.
   — If correct, she draws two more cards. She continues in this manner until she cannot make an abbreviation.
   — If incorrect, she returns the cards to her hand and her turn is over.
4. The game continues with Player 2, etc.
5. The player with the most abbreviations when all cards have been drawn wins.

State Abbreviations

Alabama	AL	Kentucky	KY	North Dakota	ND
Alaska	AK	Louisiana	LA	Ohio	OH
Arizona	AZ	Maine	ME	Oklahoma	OK
Arkansas	AR	Maryland	MD	Oregon	OR
California	CA	Massachusetts	MA	Pennsylvania	PA
Colorado	CO	Michigan	MI	Rhode Island	RI
Connecticut	CT	Minnesota	MN	South Carolina	SC
Delaware	DE	Mississippi	MS	South Dakota	SK
District of Columbia	DC	Missouri	MO	Tennessee	TN
Florida	FL	Montana	MT	Texas	TX
Georgia	GA	Nebraska	NE	Utah	UT
Hawaii	HI	Nevada	NV	Vermont	VT
Idaho	ID	New Hampshire	NH	Virginia	VA
Illinois	IL	New Jersey	NJ	Washington	WA
Indiana	IN	New Mexico	NM	West Virginia	WV
Iowa	IA	New York	NY	Wisconsin	WI
Kansas	KS	North Carolina	NC	Wyoming	WY

By the Numbers!

Writing numbers

Here's an activity that your class will number as one of its all-time favorites! Copy the patterns on page 44 for each student. Have each child label the patterns as directed on the page. Then have her cut out the patterns, color them, and add them to a bulletin board titled "By the Numbers!" After the display is complete, have each child choose a title from the board and rewrite it at the top of her paper using a different number. Then have her write a brief paragraph describing how the change in number might change the content of the song, television show, movie, or book. Add the finished paragraphs to the display.

Twenty and Ten by Claire Bishop

The 12 Days of Christmas

101 Dalmatians

Secret Message

Reading and writing abbreviations

Ex. 1

When the atty. left the bldg., he drove down Sunset Ave. to his apt.

When the attorney left the building, he drove down Sunset Avenue to his apartment.

Our teacher announced that a VIP from the FBI would visit our school today.

Ex. 2

Our teacher announced that a Very Important Person from the Federal Bureau of Investigation would visit our school today.

Take the mystery out of reading and writing abbreviations with this kid-pleasin' activity! First, provide a list of common abbreviations or have students brainstorm a list as you write their suggestions on the board. Give each student ten strips of paper. On each of five strips, have the student write a mystery message using the abbreviations provided or other abbreviations he knows (see example 1). Have the student fold each strip and place it in a container. Then have one child at a time draw a strip, read it aloud, and guess the meaning of the abbreviations.

Next, have each student label each of his five remaining strips with a sentence that includes names/phrases that could be written as initialisms (see example 2). After the student underlines each name/phrase, have him fold the strip and place it in the container. Then have one child at a time draw a slip and write its sentence on the board, substituting initialisms for the underlined words. Challenge classmates to identify what each letter stands for.

Take the Acronyms Challenge!

 Identifying acronyms

Send students sleuthing for the meanings of common acronyms with this group challenge. On the chalkboard, draw a large magnifying glass. Each morning, write in the glass one of the acronyms listed. Then challenge each cooperative group to look for the meaning in reference materials during free time or to ask family members at home that night. The next morning, give teams time to confer before turning in their answers to you. Award one point for each correct answer. Then erase the acronym and add a new one. Reward the team with the most points at the end of the challenge with no-homework coupons or another small treat.

ACRONYMS

AIDS: Acquired immune deficiency syndrome
AWOL: Absent without official leave
HUD: Housing and Urban Development
MADD: Mothers Against Drunk Driving
MASH: Mobile army surgical hospital
NASA: National Aeronautics and Space Administration
NATO: North Atlantic Treaty Organization
OPEC: Organization of Petroleum Exporting Countries
PIN: Personal identification number
RADAR: Radio detecting and ranging
SONAR: Sound navigation ranging
SWAK: Sealed with a kiss
SWAT: Special Weapons Action Team or Special Weapons and Tactics
ZIP: Zone improvement plan

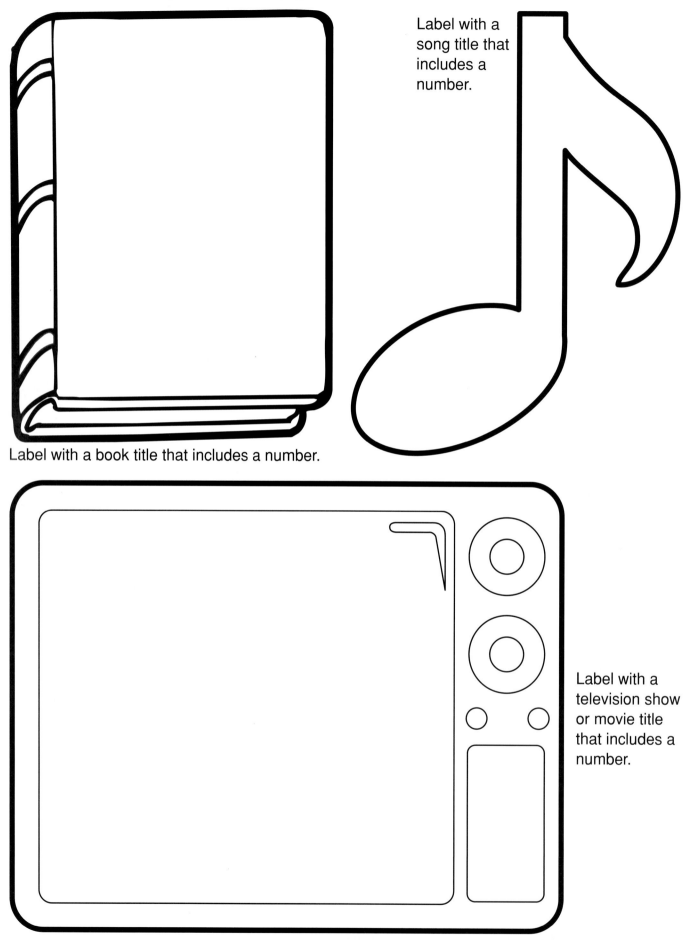

Label with a song title that includes a number.

Label with a book title that includes a number.

Label with a television show or movie title that includes a number.

Code Crackin'!

- The <u>number</u> is lucky. (15)
- He works for Crook Catchers, <u>Incorporated</u>. (5)
- I'd like to visit the Crazy Candy <u>Company</u>. (2)
- That island is located at 30 degrees <u>latitude</u>. (4)
- She lives in <u>Apartment</u> 301-B. (17)
- <u>General</u> N. Command is on TV. (11)
- He stopped at Crimestoppers <u>Avenue</u>. (1)
- Don't travel on Danger <u>Road</u>! (6)
- There are three <u>feet</u> in a yard. (13)
- Her birthday is <u>January</u> 10. (16)
- <u>President</u> E. Leck Tedd is being interviewed. (14)
- That story is <u>continued</u> on the next page. (19)
- The test is on <u>Monday</u>. (3)
- He ate almost a <u>pound</u> of cheese! (7)
- How many <u>pages</u> did we read? (9)
- The mouse weighs only a few <u>ounces</u>. (10)
- He stopped <u>inches</u> from the edge. (12)
- What <u>volume</u> did you use? (18)
- Her <u>street</u> is blocked off. (20)
- That house is creepy, scary, haunted, <u>et cetera</u>. (8)

How good are you at cracking a secret code? Find out by decoding the following secret message.

Directions: Write the abbreviation for each underlined word in the numbered blank below. Do not use periods.

I h_____ _____me to collect the _____ey. Put it in a f_____ box and _____lude a map
      1   2   3   4   5

of your location as o_____ered. Leave box at lightbu_____ factory to be f_____hed by
                              6   7   8

me. Unha_____y to report that a d_____en a_____ts are com_____g a_____er me, so I
              9   10   11   12   13

am _____sed for time. _____ word on Slim or _____ice. Think c_____ured. Too
          14   15   16   17

in_____ved to explain; details later. _____inue hiding until you hear from your si_____er.
        18   19   20

Bonus Box: Write your own secret message containing hidden abbreviations like the one above. Challenge a friend to decode it.

Cross-Country Criminal

Agents I. Sleuthmore and N. Ishall are trying to catch the notorious jewel thief Ima Crook. They made notes about their progress in the travel journal below. Write each day's number on the state or states mentioned in the journal that day. Use your social studies textbook if you need help.

Day:
1. Left VT; drove to ME.
2. Heard Crook was in MA; took a boat there.
3. Flew to VA, but got sidetracked in MD.
4. Saw her in PA.
5. Caught plane in DE.
6. Got tip Crook in SC; drove there.
7. Spotted her at Alligator World in FL.
8. Took freighter to TX, then train to OK.

Day:
9. Stopped in Branson, MO. No sign of Crook.
10. Sighted her in Omaha, NE; lost her in KS.
11. Clues she was in MN; just missed her.
12. On the trail to AK; taking plane to HI.
13. Hear she took cruise to CA.
14. Rented car in WA; drove to OR.
15. Caught her in Grand Canyon in AZ!

Not to scale

Bonus Box: On the back of this paper, write your own travel diary that describes your visit to 10 states not listed above.

Note to the teacher: If desired, let students use a United States map (one that identifies the states by name rather than postal abbreviation) to help them complete this page.

Answer Keys

Page 15

1. Lowercase
2. Zoo
3. Friday
4. Bert
5. Ernie
6. When
7. Imal
8. French
9. E.
10. October
11. Sheriff
12. Burgertime
13. Ada
14. Mrs.
15. I
16. County

Page 16

geographic names

My editor is in a meeting at the Empire State Building.

Copies of the newspaper are sent to Chicago, New York, and Miami.

names of people

That article on cooking was written by Carolyn Ames.

The sports section is edited by Sammy Slider.

titles used with names

I read Chief Garrison's report on a salary increase for police officers.

The article about Senator Jones was on the front page.

names of days and months

The sale advertisements are in the paper on Thursday.

The newspaper celebrates its 100th anniversary in July.

names of holidays

The newspaper is full of grocery store ads the week before Thanksgiving.

There will be no business section on Christmas Day.

titles of written work

Our main competitor is the *Daily Gazette*.

Magazines such as *Weekly News* are sold alongside our newspaper in newsstands.

Page 17

1. South America
2. Dr. Jones
3. *Glenwood Gazette*
4. New York
5. Christmas
6. Thursday
7. AP
8. Australian
9. December
10. President Timmons
11. *Sports Digest*
12. FBI
13. Asia
14. Civil War
15. Empire State Building
16. *Town Tribune*

Page 18

1. Brooklyn Bridge
2. New York
3. Ernest Hemingway
4. Lois Lane
5. Internal Revenue Service
6. YMCA

The byline gives the writer credit for a newspaper story.

7. Yellow River
8. Ontario
9. December
10. *Book Digest*

The body of a newspaper story answers questions for the reader.

Page 30

1. don't
2. correct
3. correct
4. correct
5. wouldn't
6. they're
7. correct
8. Jim's
9. correct
10. Captain's
11. jack-o'-lantern
12. correct
13. correct
14. correct
15. children's
16. 15's
17. correct
18. She's
19. correct
20. They'll

Your grade is __A__!

Page 33

708 Martin Street
Albion, Illinois 03928
April 5, 2000

Dear Grace,

Hi! Even though you are coming for a visit in a few weeks, I couldn't wait to tell you what happened the other day. My 14-year-old brother, the practical joker, had planned all these dumb tricks to play on me for April Fools' Day. It didn't turn out the way he planned, however, because I was ready with some tricks of my own. First, he got up early, took all my dolls, and hung them in the tree in the front yard. He then got in the shower. Well, I went out and hung a big, bright sign in the tree. It was labeled "Jason Gray's Dolls on Special Display!" Boy, was he surprised when all his friends were in the yard laughing it up! He hurried and pulled it down. He was so mad!

The next trick he tried to pull was after school. He told me that Max, the new boy from down the street, called and wanted me to call him back. He gave me the number and walked down the hall, but I knew he was hiding around the corner to listen. I knew, of course, that it was a trick to embarrass me. I dialed my friend named Beth. She has an older sister, whom Jason is *gaga* over.

I said, "Hello, this is Janet. My brother told me you called."

Beth said, "Oh, really? What's he up to?"

I could hear my brother laughing down the hall, but I tried not to smile. I replied, "Welcome to the neighborhood, Max." Beth caught on to Jason's trick, so we chatted for a minute while she pretended to be Max. My brother was still laughing. I said in a loud voice, "Oh, my brother? Your sister wants to talk to my brother?" Jason ran around the corner.

Beth got her sister on the phone. I told Jason that Max's older sister thought he was cute and wanted to talk to him. Jason took the phone. His voice squeaked out, "Hello?"

Well, you should have seen his face when he realized who was on the other end of the phone! I could see he was mad, so I started running before he got off the phone and tried to kill me. It was better than pizza, ice cream, and a big birthday check!

See you soon,
Janet

Page 34

1. Pizza—cheese or pepperoni—will be served for lunch.
2. Bring the following items to the picnic—a dessert to share, a game to play, a swimsuit, and a towel.
3. You will need six items for art class—colored pencils, markers, paintbrushes, chalk, a sketch pad, and a ruler.
4. Jason—he's my best friend—is sleeping over next weekend.
5. Each team wore a special tournament shirt—yellow or green—for the play-off game.
6. You can do one of five acts for the talent show—a dance routine, a song, a short skit, a joke-telling session, or a poetry reading.
7. My wallet—in case you hadn't noticed—is missing.
8. Lions, tigers, zebras, elephants—all can be found at the city zoo.
9. The police chief—she's my aunt's sister—will speak to my class next week.
10. The scientists say that dinosaurs are extinct, and yet—
11. For the field trip you will need these items—a bag lunch, a signed permission slip, a jacket, money for the boat ride, and your journal.
12. Soda pop—orange, grape, or root beer—will be served at the party.
13. Our favorite team—the awesome Foxville Fighting Falcons—is sure to win.
14. By June you will have learned the following—decimals, multiplication, fractions, ratios, percents, and division.
15. The following students should report to me—Jamie, Ali, Becca, Kelly, Devin, Susan, Douglas, and Flo.

Answer Keys

Page 35

1. There is a number to call if you need help with homework (800-GET-HELP).
2. The National Broadcasting Company (NBC) owns Channel 10.
3. The Society for the Prevention of Cruelty to Animals (SPCA) meets today.
4. Look for information about volcanoes in chapter 3 (pages 23–35).
5. Rosie Mallory (my neighbor) is running for state senator.
6. Mom works for the Federal Bureau of Investigation (FBI).
7. The snake we found was 60 inches (five feet) long.
8. Akeema's native country is Kenya (from which he moved when he was eight).
9. Fold the paper to resemble a butterfly (see the example).
10. Our school (Rosewood Elementary) has 362 students and 20 teachers.
11. The team members in the photo (from left to right) are Jane, Tina, and Moesha.
12. I had a 12-ounce (355 ml) box of juice for lunch today.
13. My father (who was late for work) searched everywhere for his glasses.
14. I hope my favorite team (the Dallas Cowboys®) goes to the Super Bowl®.
15. I've read my favorite book *(Tuck Everlasting)* six times already!

Answer to riddle: They just won the dinosaur tug-of-war!

Page 36

1. Please pass the salt. Thank you for your help.
2. Sheriff Wayne D. Cates investigated the robbery and caught the thieves.
3. My grandfather, Maurice O. DeMars, won't tell anyone his middle name.
4. Shanille's mother sent $3.50 to school for the field trip.
5. It will be raining this afternoon. We'll postpone the cookout.
6. The sign read "This way to Mississippi St. University," so we turned the car around.
7. John F. Kennedy was a popular U.S. president.
8. Tony spent $5.32 on baseball cards for his collection.
9. I was surprised to find out that P. J. Thomason was a girl.
10. Pay $5.00 to the ticket collector and go into the movie.
11. Take out the garbage. Do the dishes.
12. That golfer on television is Mrs. Pugh's nephew, Homer.
13. Where was Michael J. Fox born?
14. Give me the $2.25 you owe me for buying your lunch, please.
15. Dr. Flynn lives in Florida. She saw an alligator in her backyard.
16. The soccer team practices on Saturday. They practice in all kinds of weather.
17. I heard Ms. Conway wrecked a golf cart last Friday.
18. The dog dug a hole for his bone. He dug it up later in the day.

Page 37

"Hi, Pat and Lea," said Micah.

"Hey, Micah," Pat said. "What's up?"

Micah answered, "You won't believe what my grandmother gave me for my birthday!"

"What?" Lea asked.

"Guess," Micah responded.

"Well," Pat said, "how about giving us a few hints?"

"Good idea!" Lea agreed.

"Okay," Micah answered, smiling. "Let's see. It's something I've always wanted."

"That's not much of a clue," Pat laughed. "It could be anything."

"It's something I'll have lots of fun with," Micah added.

Lea said, "That narrows it down to about a million things! Add some details."

Micah continued, "It's about 10 inches high and 20 inches long. It feels good to touch. It uses a lot of energy. I'll have to take good care of it. My mom said I can keep it in my room. Now, guess what it is."

Lea and Pat said together, "It's a _____!"

(Answers about what the gift is may vary, depending on the reasons stated by the students. Most students will likely respond that the gift is a dog or a cat.)

Page 45

I h**ave** **come** to collect the m**one**y. Put it in a f**la**t box and **include** a map of your location as **or**dered. Leave box at lightbu**lb** factory to be **fe**tched by me. Unha**ppy** to report that a d**oze**n a**gen**ts are com**ing** **af**ter me, so I am pr**esse**d for time. **No** word on Slim or **Jan**ice. Think c**ap**tured. Too inv**olve**d to explain; details later. **Con**tinue hiding until you hear from your sis**te**r.

Page 46

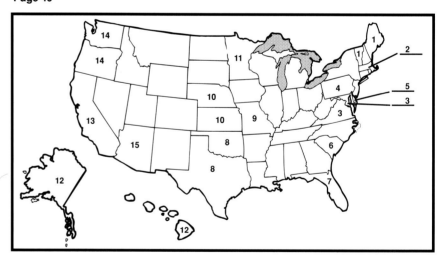

From Your Friends At The MAILBOX®

Must-Have Books for Intermediate Teachers

The Best of *The Mailbox*® Language Arts

For grades 4–6, this comprehensive resource from *The MAILBOX*® magazine is brimming with motivational units covering everything from parts of speech to spelling to vocabulary enrichment and lots more. Whether you're in your first year or a pro, you'll love having the tools you need in one easy-to-use book. 160 pages.

TEC 1460. The Best of *The MAILBOX*® Language Arts (Grades 4-6)

The Best of *The Mailbox*® Math

Energize your math lessons and strengthen students' math skills with this timesaving collection of units from *The MAILBOX*® magazine. You'll find helpful ideas for math centers, manipulatives and games, class projects, literature links, reproducibles, patterns, and more. 176 pages.

TEC 849. The Best of *The MAILBOX*® Math (Grades 4-6)

The Best of *The Mailbox*® Literature

Enrich your curriculum with teacher-tested ideas based on classic children's literature. The Best of *The MAILBOX*® Literature features novel units, literature-based theme units with across-the-curriculum activities, a bonanza of book report ideas, motivating ideas for getting kids into books, and much more. 160 pages.

TEC 1464. The Best of *The MAILBOX*® Literature (Grades 4-6)

Science Made Simple

From outer space to inner earth, this book has the science units you're looking for. Science Made Simple is an easy-to-use collection of hands-on science activities and projects taken directly from the pages of *The Intermediate Mailbox*® magazine. Units include earthquakes, magnetism & electricity, the five senses, weather, whales, and rocks & minerals. Grades 4–6.

TEC 847. The Best of *The MAILBOX*® Science Made Simple, Book 1 (Grades 4-6) 176 pages

TEC 1475. The Best of *The MAILBOX*® Science Made Simple, Book 2 (Grades 4-6) 160 pages

The Best of *The Mailbox*®—Intermediate

Book 1: A valuable resource book created especially for teachers of grades 4–6. The Book 1 edition contains our editors' favorite classroom-tested ideas and activities from the first decade of *The* Intermediate *Mailbox*®. 192 pages.

TEC 841. The Best of *The* Intermediate *Mailbox*® Book 1 (Grs. 4-6)

Book 2: Our Book 2 represents the editors' selections from more recent years of *The* Intermediate *Mailbox*®. We've included popular magazine features such as "Our Readers Write" and "Lifesavers... Management Tips For Teachers." 192 pages.

TEC 846. The Best of *The* Intermediate *Mailbox*® Book 2 (Grs. 4-6)

Book 3: This volume is an indispensable treasure chest of practical, age-appropriate, creative classroom ideas that are fun for students and easy for teachers. Teachers will find creative teaching units, literature activities, management tips, bulletin-board ideas, art projects, reproducibles, patterns, and much more. 192 pages.

TEC 835. The Best of *The* Intermediate *Mailbox*® Book 3 (Grs. 4-6)

Exploring Social Studies— Book 1 & 2

China, immigration, map skills, the Civil War—these are just a few of the interesting social studies units you'll find in *Exploring Social Studies*. This collection features a wide array of social studies units first featured in *The* Intermediate *MAILBOX*® magazine. Our editors have included critical-thinking activities, literature selections, reproducibles, arts-and-crafts activities, plus many more features to enhance your social studies curriculum.

TEC 848. The Best of *The MAILBOX*® Exploring Social Studies, Book 1 (Grades 4-6) 176 pages.

TEC 1474. The Best of *The MAILBOX*® Exploring Social Studies, Book 2 (Grades 4-6) 160 pages

From Your Friends at **The MAILBOX®**

Grammar Plus!

Capitalization & Punctuation

Motivating Activities to Teach Basic Skills

Hook your students on using good grammar with creative lessons on capitalization, punctuation, and mechanics that make learning grammar fun! With this collection of easy-to-implement ideas and reproducibles, you'll find just the lesson you need to teach basic grammar and mechanics skills.

This book and the others in this series help you add pizzazz to those boring old grammar rules so you can help your students master good grammar once and for all. Your students will understand when to use punctuation marks and will pay attention to capitalization like never before! Teach them how to spot bad grammar and what to do to correct those errors. They'll gain confidence in their writing. You'll see the results in their everyday communications and in their test scores. No more boring grammar lessons! No more bad grammar!

Included in this book:

- abbreviations
- apostrophes
- acronyms
- commas
- dashes
- exclamation points
- hyphens
- parentheses
- semicolons

And much more!

Also available:

TEC2314. Grammar Plus! Sentence Structure & Usage
TEC2315. Grammar Plus! Parts of Speech

www.themailbox.com

ISBN 1-56234-389-0

7 21202 02313 9